MIDDLE EASTERN
FOOD AND DRINK

Christine Osborne

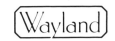

FOOD AND DRINK

British Food and Drink
Chinese Food and Drink
French Food and Drink
Greek Food and Drink
Indian Food and Drink

Italian Food and Drink
Japanese Food and Drink
Middle Eastern Food and Drink
Russian Food and Drink
Spanish Food and Drink

Editor: Jillie Norrey

First published in 1988 by
Wayland (Publishers) Limited
61 Western Road, Hove
East Sussex BN3 1JD, England

© Copyright 1988 Wayland (Publishers) Limited

British Library Cataloguing in Publication Data
Osborne, Christine
   Middle Eastern food and drink.—
   (Food and drink).
   1. Cookery, Middle Eastern—Juvenile
   literature   2. Beverages—Middle East
   —Juvenile literature
   I. Title   II. Series
   641'.0956   TX725.N36

ISBN 1–85210–313–2

Typeset by DP Press, Sevenoaks
Printed in Italy by G. Canale & C.S.p.A., Turin
Bound in France by A.G.M.

Cover *A suq in the Sultanate of Oman. In many countries in the Middle East it is customary for men to do the shopping.*

Contents

The Middle East and its people

The Middle East covers an area of over 17 million square km, stretching between the north-eastern shoulder of Africa and south-west Asia (see map). The fourteen countries in the region have many different forms of government, but there is only one main religion – Islam. The word 'Islam' means 'submission to God'.

The founder of Islam was an Arab named Muhammad. Born in Makkah, Saudi Arabia, he experienced a series of divine messages from God, via the Angel Gabriel. When local tribes raised objections to his teachings, Muhammad and his followers migrated inland, to Madinah. This migration, or *hijra* in Arabic, was the first day of the Muslim calendar, AD 622.

Islam means 'submission to God'. Facing the holy city of Makkah, an Arab prays in the dunes of Abu Dhabi.

In Madinah, Islam quickly grew into an organized religious force which managed to recapture Makkah in AD 630. After the death of Muhammad, his followers, or Muslims, carefully transcribed his thoughts into a holy book known as the Qur'an. This remains the code for righteous living for Muslims all over the world.

In AD 632, Muslim armies overran the Middle East. Their vast empire was ruled by successive caliphates – first, the Ummayads (AD 660) in Damascus and later the Abbasids who transferred the capital to Baghdad in AD 762. When Baghdad

4

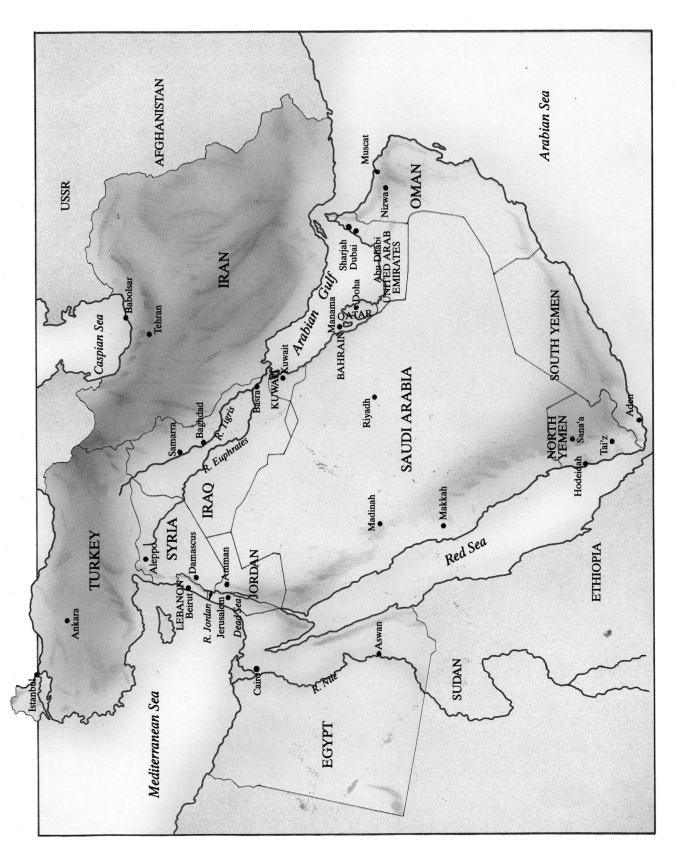

fell to the Mongols in the thirteenth century, the Islamic empire broke into rival caliphates. The Fatimid dynasty in Cairo was the most famous of these caliphates.

Christian armies tried to capture the Holy Land, but the Muslim leader, Salah al-Din, restored it to Muslim rule in AD 1187.

By the sixteenth century, the Ottomans were a powerful force in the Middle East. In 1516, they took Cairo and extended their influence throughout the region. Following their defeat in World War I, former Ottoman-Turkish colonies were divided between Britain and France. It was not until after the end of World War II (1945) that foreign rule ended under rising Arab nationalism. The last area to obtain independence as a sovereign state was the Trucial States which merged to form the United Arab Emirates in 1971.

The population of the Middle East exceeds 100 million and can be divided into three groups: the Bedouin nomads, the farmers and the townspeople.

Once practised by a majority, pastoral nomadism is likely to die out. Better living standards, housing and education sees many

Bedouin watering their flock at a tank in Syria. Nomadism is becoming rare as families settle down.

Bedouin settling down. The change is rapid in the Arab oil-states able to offer generous welfare schemes but slower in less well off countries such as Jordan, Syria and Iraq where seasonal migrations still continue. Contact with the farming community plays an important part in encouraging the Bedouin to change their nomadic ways.

About half the people in the Middle East are farmers, or *hadhar*. Agricultural work usually involves the entire family. Farming is still mainly performed using traditional methods such as harvesting by hand sickle; as a result living standards are low.

Most governments encourage co-operative projects by giving money for fertilizers and mechanized cultivators. Except in the Arab states with huge sums of money to spend on hi-tech farming projects, progress is slow.

The third group, the towns-people, are historically associated with commerce and the crafts, and traditionally work in the *suq*, or market.

In many rapidly developing cities, commerce has overflowed from the *suq* into new parts of town. Western-type offices, shops and supermarkets have sprung up, but traditional *suq* life continues in old Arab cities such as Cairo, Baghdad and Damascus.

Vast differences exist between the economies of the fourteen countries that make up the Middle East.

This former nomad and his wife have started farming. The tractor is shared.

Egypt probably has the best balance between industry and agriculture. Some, like North Yemen, practise subsistence farming and rely, to a large degree, on money earned by nationals working abroad. Oil and gas producers such as Saudi Arabia, Dubai and Qatar have branched into industries such as steel, aluminium, chemicals and paints. Tiny states such as Ajman and Umm al Qawain exist solely on support from their rich neighbours.

Food – yesterday and today

The origins of Middle Eastern food can be traced back to early Bedouin and peasant dishes.

The nomadic habit of moving from place to place made cultivation and the preparation of elaborate meals difficult. We know that bread figured in their diet by the discovery of stone querns for grinding wheat which were shared by various migrating tribes. Pulses were almost certainly eaten following contact with peasant farmers.

One of the oldest-known foods are figs, which thrive in a poor soil and are thought to have been

Egyptian bas-reliefs indicate what was eaten thousands of years ago. Fish, honey and pelicans' eggs were popular.

cultivated for as long as 5 000 years. Dates and melons, originally from Persia (now Iran), and Afghanistan, also date from around this time. Grapes, which are native to Persia, have been eaten for a very long time. The Bible tells us that lentils, chick peas and other pulses were eaten by the Egyptians. Still enjoyed, the green, spinach-like soup called *melokhia* originates from the time of the Pharaohs. Egyptian bas-reliefs depicting bee-hives indicate that honey was popular. Ducks', pelicans' and ostrich eggs were also eaten in biblical times.

Culinary records exist from the twelfth century, but further knowledge of foods in early Middle Eastern cuisine remains locked in ancient recipe books awaiting translation. One of the best references is *al-Kitab al Wusla il al-Habib* written by Muhammad al-Baghdadi during the declining days of Abbasid rule in Baghdad. Many of the dishes he describes belonged to the exotic court cuisine of the Abbasid caliphate (AD 750-1258).

Social Life Under the Abbasids translated by Muhammad Manazir Ahsan gives interesting information on food and drink under the second Islamic caliphate.

Vegetables were greatly prized. Garlic was an important ingredient and asparagus was so popular that

Baghdad, 'City of a Thousand and One Nights' was the capital of the Abbasid caliphate (AD 750-1258).

poems were written describing its qualities. Aubergine, or *badhinjan*, figured in many different recipes. The Caliph Wathiq was so fond of it, he used to eat forty at a time!

From the same period in history, *The Tales of A Thousand And One Nights* throws more light on ancient diet. We learn that chickens were roasted in 'clarified cow-butter' and meat casseroles flavoured with cumin were popular. Fatima, wife of Ma'Aruf, a Cairene cobbler, preferred *knaffeh* (vermicelli sweetmeat) made with bees' honey much more than with cane honey.

In another tale we read of a memorable dinner when '. . . there (were) rice of several colours, and sherbets of as many more; and kids stuffed with walnuts and almonds and pistachios, and a camel-colt roasted whole . . .'

Faludhaj a Persian concoction made from marzipan and rose-water-flavoured dough is one of the oldest known sweetmeats in the Middle East. It is believed to have been created for pilgrims to take with them on the *hajj*, or pilgrimage, to the holy city of Makkah, in Saudi Arabia. Still made today, *zalabiya*, a tart filled with almonds, sugar and flavoured with rose-water or musk is also mentioned by Ahsan.

Many Middle Eastern recipes

Ever-popular, knaffeh *is a rich sweetmeat mentioned in the* Tales of a Thousand and One Nights.

Mansaf, *a lamb and rice dish, is typical of Bedouin cuisine in the Levant (Syria, Jordan and Lebanon).*

have survived unchanged for hundreds of years, despite influence from foreign dishes. *Mansaf* (chunks of stewed lamb, doused with yoghurt and served on a bed of rice), for example, is straight out of Bedouin life in Jordan and Syria. Yemeni dishes are as pure as ever; *Zahawiq*, a dip made from tomato pulp, chillis and tiny dried fish, is unique to this remote corner of the Arabian peninsula. *Saluf bi-hilbeh* (flat bread spread with coriander and fenugreek paste) is another medieval-tasting snack to be found in this fascinating country.

However, as Westernized ingredients have become available (commerically manufactured *ghee*, for instance – as opposed to traditional *samneh*) other dishes have lost their original taste. Higher grade imported meat and poultry has also improved many recipes without any basic change.

Recipes in Middle Eastern cooking are passed down from mother to daughter. Watching the preparation of food and participating in the cooking remains a traditional aspect of female society. In former times, when many people were illiterate, this method was the only way. And still today, when compared to the West, there are not many recipe books in Arabic.

As in Western countries, costly and time consuming recipes are disappearing. Served on special occasions, the famous Arab *khouzi* is an example. Not only is it very expensive (a whole sheep stuffed with chickens, eggs, rice and pinenuts), it requires a king-size oven, or *tanour* to cook for hours.

Other early victims have been desserts and sweetmeats. Similar to a Western housewife who no longer makes her grandmother's recipe for coconut-ice, a Middle Eastern housewife now sends out to the *suq*, for *lokum* (Turkish delight) and *halwa* (semolina and nut slice).

Fresh bread is also bought daily from the baker, often by the man returning home for lunch. Strangely enough, as Westerners develop a taste for unleavened bread, there is a trend in some Arab cities towards sliced white bread and long French loaves.

Trays of lokum, *or Turkish delight, outside a sweet shop in old Jerusalem.*

Growing the food

Mount Damavand, the highest mountain in the Middle East.

The Middle East is characterized by areas of desert in the south, particularly in the Arabian peninsula and by rugged mountain ranges in the Levant – Syria, Jordan Lebanon – and in Iran. The highest peak is Mount Damavand (5 671 m) in Iran, while the lowest point is the Dead Sea in Jordan, some 400 m below sea-level.

The entire region has a very hot summer (June-October) without rain. Winter (November-March) varies from very cold with snow, to dry and warm in southern Arabia.

There is a huge variation in rainfall. The Levant receives reliable rain, usually between December and April, but two-thirds of the Arabian peninsula depends on cloudbursts. In countries such as Kuwait and the United Arab Emirates, the desalination of seawater is essential, not only for farming, but for people to survive.

Lack of water, the severe climate and a generally poor, stony soil, are historic problems associated with the cultivation of food in the Middle East. The discovery of simple agricultural tools in Jordan and Iraq, do, however, indicate farming from around 5000 BC.

The ancient Egyptians and Mesopotamians displayed great flair at dam building and the construction of canals permitting the irrigation of former wasteland. The Mesopotamians are credited with the invention of the *shadouf*, a pulley and bucket form of irrigation: a variation is still in use.

Like Egypt's Aswan High Dam irrigating the Nile river valley and Jordan's East Ghor Canal scheme feeding the east bank of the river Jordan, Iraq's agricultural programme currently centres on the Tharthar reservoir, near the historic town of Samarra.

Egypt and the countries of the Levant are the biggest food producers in the Middle East. The main cereals grown are wheat and pulses. Most vegetables are cultivated and the citrus fruit crop is exceptional. Other fruits are peaches, grapes, melons, bananas

Hi-tech agriculture is practised in the oil-rich Gulf states. Qatar, where this picture was taken, is a pioneer in hydroponic irrigation.

and pomegranates. Syria and Iran produce high grade almonds, walnuts and pistachio nuts. Biblical foods such as olives and dates also do well. The sub-tropical south coast of Oman produces mangoes and coconuts.

The Arab oil-states still rely heavily on imported foods, but great advances have been made in agriculture. Using hydroponic techniques, many Arab countries produce their own tomatoes, beans, cabbages and courgettes. The state of Qatar, which is 95 per cent desert, maintains a dairy herd producing 5 tonnes of milk a day. Fodder, vegetables and cereals are grown on an area of 1 000 sq m under irrigation.

Several countries in the Middle East are self-sufficient in seafood supplied by local fishermen. Upgrading fishing techniques will revolutionize production.

Lamb, the basic meat, has been raised since biblical times. Other meat requirements are imported. Most countries are now self-sufficient in poultry and eggs.

Fishermen still weave traditional wire traps in Bahrain. Upgrading methods will improve the catch.

Selling the food

Transport to the market

Medieval methods of transporting goods to market remain common in the Middle East.

Donkeys are faithful 'beasts of burden' in rugged areas inaccessible to motor vehicles, such as the central highlands of North Yemen. Camels still transport dates and fish along the Red Sea coast. As well as being used for ploughing in poor areas in the Levant, mules carry loads to the *suqs*.

Elsewhere, improved standards of living and communications enable farm produce to be taken to town by truck – generally a Toyota pick-up van. The lack of refrigeration facilities throughout the Middle East means that quick transportation of goods likely to

A farmer ploughing in the highlands of North Yemen. Donkeys still have many uses in the rugged parts of the Middle East.

perish quickly, such as fish and fruits, is vital. Often there is a rural depot from where goods make the final journey from the farm to the market in a town. Either way, the *suq* opens shortly after the first prayer; by noon the choicest goods are sold.

The *suq* (market)

Found in every Middle Eastern city, the pattern or layout of the *suq* developed during the expansion of Islam in the seventh century AD. Then, and today, craftsmen and specialized food vendors all group together: silversmiths, carpenters, perfume blenders, bakers, greengrocers, spice sellers and so on.

The *suq* is always in the centre of a town, or in the case of rapidly expanding cities such as Riyadh or Dubai, in what used to be the centre. Shops are grouped around the mosque for the traders' convenience at prayer times. The huge al-Hamadieh *suq* in Damascus surrounds the magnificent, ancient Ummayad mosque. The Great Mosque in Sana'a, capital of North Yemen, is enclosed by the *suq*.

One can recognize the various trades in the *suq* even with the eyes closed. The sharp noise made by the coffee-seller dropping his beans onto a set of brass scales, the rattle as the nut-seller plunges his spoon

Above *Children traditionally help their father. In this picture, boys look after a nut stall in the great al-Hamadieh* suq *in Damascus, Syria.*

A Palestinian woman shopping in the suq *in old Jerusalem. Although colourful, most* suqs *are crowded and poorly lit.*

into a sack of walnuts, the butcher chopping chunks of meat, sneezing in the *attarine* or spice street as people sample cumin and paprika, and the water-seller ringing his bell.

While a *suq* enables a backward glance at the traditional Middle East, in the developing world it seems to belong to another time. There is very little space; the streets are often unpaved, poorly lit and congested with pedestrians and mules. In the oil-rich Arab states, many old *suqs* have been demolished. Sharjah's old 'Arabian style' *suq* is now relocated with other trades. Abu Dhabi's open *suq* has changed into a series of supermarkets and cold stores.

Whether working outside or inside, in most cases the traders are men. An exception is seen in towns like Sana'a and Ta'iz in North Yemen where veiled women are found selling vegetables and eggs. At lunch hour in Sana'a, groups of women also sell bread outside the restaurants from round, flat baskets carried on their heads.

In some countries a woman will do the shopping, accompanied by a friend, or a male member of the household. In the strictly traditional Arabian states, however, shopping is a man's job. Especially on Thursday morning, before the Friday rest day, the *suq* in Kuwait is filled with husbands doing the 'weekend shopping'. Where supermarkets are replacing *suqs*, as in Doha, capital of Qatar, women are finally starting to shop, but still usually in a group rather than alone.

Within the *suq* are various associated snack bars selling things like *falafel* (fried lentil patties) and *shawarma* (skewered lamb). Boiled eggs and potatoes are sold on upturned packing cases in Sana'a while the *limoonada* (or lemonade) trolley is a feature of Cairo's crowded market place. Jerusalem has a coffee-seller announcing his presence by rattling his cups like castanets.

In the old days parades through *suqs* were common. Not simply for entertainment, but to demonstrate the importance of local commerce and crafts.

In many Arab states, a man does the shopping. Here, a woman follows her husband round the suq *in Kuwait.*

Shawarma, *or skewered slices of lamb, seen here turning slowly on a vertical grill, is a popular snack.*

One such parade, described by a French visitor to seventeenth century Aleppo, included splendid floats carried by bearers on which bakers were rolling dough and a company of confectioners who were carrying castles of sugar on their heads. All the craftsmen, as well as traders, were represented – there were cobblers, tailors and dyers and, in order of social and economic importance, coffee-sellers, spice merchants and butchers.

The fish market may be in a separate section of the main *suq*, or it may be quite apart. In Muscat, Oman, and Hodeidah on the Red Sea coast of North Yemen, the catch is sold direct from the boats. Baskets of huge Gulf prawns are sold by auction in Bahrain. The caviar industry is long established and well organized in Iran with headquarters at Babolsar on the Caspian Sea.

Bread is sold direct from the baker, hot out of the huge clay oven, or *tanour*. As times change, it is also found packaged in supermarkets.

Tribesmen buy fish fresh off the boat in the Sultanate of Oman.

The nutritional value of food

The nutritional value of Middle Eastern food is very high. The cholesterol level is low. Vegetable oils such as olive oil, groundnut and safflower oil are the main mediums used for cooking. Grills are popular, rich sauces are uncommon. Among the poorer people, meat still remains a luxury food. Fish, which is of particular importance in a well balanced diet, is widely eaten.

While there is a modern trend towards buying frozen foods, most people prefer fresh – even if this means shopping in the hot, crowded *suq*. If you watch a servant shopping somewhere like the vegetable market in old Jerusalem – you will see how carefully she inspects each tomato or aubergine, sniffing it and turning it over in her hand. People place great emphasis on the quality of fruits and vegetables. Unlike in Western shops, few would dream of buying tired old items at a bargain price.

Fresh salads and a vegetable dish are always served with a meal. Rice replaces the starchy potatoes prominent in Europe. Yoghurt is eaten in copious quantities. Bread is made from wholemeal, stone-ground flour. Butter is used in cooking in the clarified form of

Fish is popular in Arabia. Markets begin trading at dawn after the first prayer-call.

Pistachio nut cultivation in central Syria. Nuts are common ingredients in many Middle Eastern recipes.

samneh, or ghee, from which impurities have been strained. Tea and coffee are taken without milk.

The fat content in most foods is therefore low. Nuts provide body-building proteins, the most commonly used being almonds, pinenuts, walnuts and pistachios. Nuts contain traces of many important elements such as phosphorus, calcium, iron, magnesium, potassium, Vitamins E and B, plus they contain healthy quantities of fibre. Honey is widely eaten in sweetmeats. 'Fast' foods like chips and hot dogs are unheard of!

Superstitions surround several foods. Eating honey and syrups is considered to make life sweeter and to ward off the *djinn* (devil). Garlic is also supposed to guard against evil. The rich Syrian dessert called *ma'mounia* is eaten, smothered in cream, by a woman hoping to regain her strength after child-birth. The Prophet Muhammad considered that eating pomegranate cleared the body of impurities.

Cooking and special ingredients

To prepare Middle Eastern food, you only really need one or two items in addition to basic kitchen equipment.

In the Middle East, most cooks still use a traditional pestle and mortar (*maddaqa* and *jorn*) for the many grinding jobs, such as making *kibbeh* – ground lamb and *burghul* (cracked wheat). It is still advisable to have a pestle and mortar, preferably made of stone, for grinding small amounts of spices and garlic, but a modern, multi-purpose mixer makes life much easier for the cook. The old type of cast-iron garlic press is also useful as both garlic and onion are widely used in recipes.

In the Middle East there are many hands to help with the preparation of meals – families live together in an extended unit usually with grannies, aunts and so on. A grandmother may spend hours chopping the parsley for *tabbouleh* salad. She has little else to do and cooking is a time for socializing among women who do not have meeting places such as the male coffee-house. A Western cook can use an electric chopper for the task; likewise a blender attachment for making soups and beverages.

A deep frying pan and heavy based saucepans are best for cooking. Have skewers available for grilling kebabs. A large, round baking tray, known as a *sanieh* in the Middle East, is useful for baking together with shallow, flat trays for making sweetmeats. Finally, keep a piece of muslin handy for straining yoghurt and squeezing water out of soaked *burghul*.

Kibbeh, *or ground meat patties, are widely eaten throughout the Middle East. Stuffed* kibbeh, *seen here, is a Syrian speciality.*

Special ingredients

Although it is expensive, olive oil is widely used in Middle Eastern cooking. Vegetable oils such as corn and nut oils can be substituted, but where a recipe especially calls for olive oil, as well as when the dish is to be served chilled, it is essential to the flavour.

Many rural cooks continue to use homemade *samneh*, however, *ghee*,

now sold commercially, is a reasonable substitute.

Other stock items for cooking Middle Eastern food are a good supply of *burghul*, *tahini* (sesame seed paste), lentils, chick peas, lots of lemon and parsley, various nuts especially walnuts and pistachio nuts and scented water for flavourings and spices.

Spices

The subtle addition of spices is a characteristic of Middle Eastern foods. They are bought, as required, in small amounts from the local *attarine*, or spice street, in the *suq*. For the correct flavour, you should only use fresh amounts.

Many spices are native to the Middle East. The most widely used

Fresh spices are purchased in small amounts in the attarine, *or spice street. Pictured here is a spice shop in Ta'iz, North Yemen.*

is cumin whose delicate aroma adds flavour to many salads and vegetable dishes. Whole or ground cumin is also added to the curried seafood popular in Arab countries. *Baharat* (a mixture of cumin, coriander, cloves, cinnamon, nutmeg and paprika) is a special ingredient in dishes from Iraq and the Arabian Gulf States.

The Middle East is the world's biggest importer of cardamom. Ground cardamom complements many meat dishes. It is also added to sweeten recipes while its pods give Arab coffee its distinctive aroma and taste.

Cloves and cinnamon add a

haunting flavour to many dishes while coriander, another plant native to the Middle East, is widely used. Ginger and nutmeg have been featured in Middle Eastern recipes since medieval times, the latter as a garnish on desserts.

Paprika, or capsicum, is a popular ingredient in many casseroles and salads. The hotter chilli is restricted to cooking in the Gulf States and in particular in Yemen, in fiery-tasting dishes such as *hilbeh* (a local dip).

Sesame seed is an historic spice in the Middle East. Raw, or roasted, its seeds add zest to breads. The oil is used on salads and in *tahini* (a combination of toasted sesame seed, garlic and lemon-juice blended into a paste). *Tahini* always features in a *mezze*, or table of appetisers. Anise, saffron and fenugreek are other spices used in Middle Eastern cooking. A glossary of the most common spices appears on page 45.

Serving

You can serve Middle Eastern food on normal Western dinner-ware. *Mezze* are ideally presented on small, oval-shaped plates, either chrome, china or glass. Dips look best in earthenware, or pottery bowls. Salads are attractive in glass bowls. To serve coffee the local way, use a long-handled brass coffee-pot or *rakwi*. It is drunk from tiny china cups without handles, or in tiny glasses set in brass holders. If the hands are used for eating, a servant or bearer may bring perfumed water which is poured over your hands into a bowl as a rinse. While it is traditional to eat with the right hand, Western style cutlery is becoming more common.

The Arab coffee ceremony is a complex ritual. Twigs in the spout help to strain the thick, black brew.

The meals and customs

It is hard to generalize about diet in the Middle East. What people eat is very much linked to their social and economic situation.

Breakfast for a Bedouin herdsman may consist only of coffee and bread. Likewise a bowl of soup must sustain a farmer in wintry parts of Jordan or Iraq, until the evening meal.

On the other hand, a well-travelled, urban business couple living in Beirut, Baghdad or Amman, may take a continental-style, or even an English breakfast (except for bacon which is forbidden by the Qur'an).

Lunch for the city dweller might be a pitta bread sandwich of

'Pocket-bread' sandwiches are popular lunch-time snacks for office workers in Cairo and other Middle Eastern cities.

shawarma (spitted lamb) and salad. When offices close early in summer, the main meal is eaten in the mid-afternoon. Since this consists of several courses, dinner at night (9 pm–10 pm) is light, often left-overs and fruit.

While availability, quality and quantity all play a part in the local diet, customs surrounding eating habits are universal. The Qur'an contains common dietary laws for all Muslims, no matter what their rank or status in the community.

Whether a family is gathered

round a humble cloth on the floor, or seated at a Western-style dinner table, it is customary for men to have the first choice of the food. In traditional Arab society, in parts of Saudi Arabia and the Gulf States, women may eat apart from male members of the family.

A meal in the Middle East begins with someone, usually the head of the family, giving thanks to Allah, or God, the provider – 'Bismillah!'

Portions of food are taken only with the right hand (the left being reserved for cleansing and washing the person). Pieces of bread are used for the dips and to pick up morsels. A guest should accept graciously choice pieces offered by the host.

Arabs, in particular, do not talk much while they are eating with the result that meals are often hurried affairs. It is considered impolite to speak with the mouth full, to stop eating when others have not finished or to display the soles of the feet if seated on the floor. Shoes, of course, are removed before entering a Muslim house.

When the meal is finished, the

Humble families eat off a cloth spread on the floor. Men always have first choice of the food.

Enjoying a mezze *at the Kuwait Hilton. Only the right hand is used for eating.*

hands are washed by a servant pouring water over them into a bowl. In urban homes, it is the custom to move to another room for coffee, a *nargila*, or water-pipe (men only), and conversation.

In more progressive cities, such as Amman, Cairo, Damascus and Beirut, a family outing, or lunch, is a Thursday night, or Friday tradition. Modern families wear Western clothes and like to dine at one of the smart hotels, or restaurants. They may order a French-type menu, but will always start with *mezze*.

Entertainment may be provided by a local singer, belly-dancer, or by an Italian, Filipino or other imported band.

Local society weddings are always held in the best hotels. Never a week passes in Cairo without a traditional marriage feast for as many as 500 guests at the Nile Hilton, or the beautiful Mena House Oberoi at the Pyramids.

Traditional food

We have seen that Middle Eastern food is composed of many different cuisines, primarily Phoenician, Persian, Arab and Ottoman-Turk. While there are regional variations and preferences, certain dishes are eaten by most peoples.

Bread accompanies every meal. It is made in various shapes and sizes – huge loaves like the Persian

A baker in Manama, capital of Bahrain. Flat, unleavened bread, or khoubz, *is baked in a traditional clay oven, or* tanour.

barbari, long, crusty loaves, or *kaik tawil* from Jordan, and *lahuh*, a sour dough bread eaten in Yemen. *Khoubz*, or round, flat bread is the most common.

Several foods are characteristic. These are *mezze* (which always include several dips), salads and sweetmeats. Main courses follow a meat, poultry or fish theme depending on availability.

Generally considered a Lebanese creation, *mezze*, or appetizers, are eaten in many countries. In Iran, they are known as *pish ghaza*.

Often displaying as many as forty to fifty different dishes, a *mezze* table is something to look forward to and to be discussed for days afterwards.

Mezze can either be hors d'oeuvres such as olives, radishes and white cheese or plates of miniature main courses. Fried liver, brains, calamare, grilled chicken wings, lentil and meat patties and *kibbeh* (ground meat and *burghul* rissoles) are typical.

Creamy dips are the highlight of a *mezze* table. The most traditional are *hummus*, made from puréed chick peas and *tahini* (sesame seed paste), *babagannouj* (grilled, puréed aubergine mixed with *tahini*), yoghurt, or *labneh*, and *taramasalata*, (puréed mullet, or cod roe).

Tabbouleh,   artichoke   hearts,

Hummus

You will need:

180 g of chick peas
1 teaspoon of sodium bicarbonate
1-2 garlic cloves
a pinch of salt
140 g of *tahini*
juice of 2-3 lemons
3 tablespoons of olive oil
paprika and finely chopped parsley as
  garnish

What to do:

Soak the chick peas overnight in a saucepan of cold water. (1) Drain, add the sodium bicarbonate and cook in a pressure-cooker for about 20 minutes (or simmer for 1-2 hours in a saucepan). Drain the chick peas, reserve the liquid and keep aside a few peas as garnish. (2) Using a little of the liquid, reduce the chick peas to a purée in a blender. Add the garlic, salt and *tahini* and blend thoroughly. (3) Finally add the lemon juice to obtain a rich, creamy consistency. (4) Pour into a shallow dish, pour the oil in the centre and garnish with the whole chick peas. Sprinkle a little paprika and chopped parsley around the edge as decoration.
Serves 6.

Hummus should be served at room temperature. Use Arab bread as a dip. It is also tasty eaten with kebabs.

Safety note: If you are using a pressure-cooker, ask an adult to operate it for you.

celery and stuffed vine leaves always feature in a *mezze* which is laid out like a Swedish smorgasbord or buffet. Cocktail sticks are used for spearing items such as mussels. Pieces of bread are used to wrap around *tabbouleh* and for the dips.

Arak, or *raki*, an anise-based drink, is traditionally provided for

Creamy hummus *dip and* tabbouleh *salad are two of the most popular appetisers served as* mezze.

guests who are not forbidden by their religion from drinking alcohol. At a big *mezze* no main course is served.

The measure by which a good cook is often judged is on her skill at preparing the time consuming *mezze* and her talent for making *kibbeh*. Small, egg-shaped rissoles stuffed with ground lamb and pinenuts, *kibbeh* are the most traditional meat dish in the Middle East, in particular in the Levant (Syria, Lebanon and Jordan). They can be eaten hot, or cold, with a selection of dips such as *hummus* and *muhammara* (puréed capsicum and walnuts).

Many Middle Eastern recipes feature ground meat (minced meat) because local lamb is often tough. Charcoal-grilled ground meat kebabs and vegetables such as aubergines, courgettes, marrows and cabbages stuffed with ground meat, are traditionally popular. Meat is often casseroled with okra and beans. Better cuts are kept for *kebabs* and the more elaborate dishes such as boned neck of lamb with rice and raisin stuffing.

Offal is popular. Brains, sweetbreads, kidneys and liver are all favourites.

Ancient recipe manuals list over 300 different ways of cooking chicken in the Middle East.

Among traditional chicken dishes are lemon chicken casserole, roast chicken stuffed with rice and pinenuts and boiled chicken pieces

Ground meat kebabs

You will need:

1 kg of lean minced lamb, or beef
3 medium onions, finely chopped
6 tablespoons of coarsely chopped
  parsley
salt and freshly ground black pepper
½ teaspoon of allspice
½ teaspoon of cayenne pepper
flour for dusting
oil for brushing

What to do:

(1) Put the meat, onions and other ingredients through a food processor until well combined. (2) With moist hands, break off walnut-sized lumps of the mixture and mould into sausage shapes around a skewer (two per skewer). (3) Dust with the flour to hold in place, brush lightly with the oil and cook under a pre-heated grill, turning frequently (a barbecue is ideal). (4) Serve on a platter lined with lettuce leaves and with a sliced lemon to garnish. Eat with rice and a salad.
Serves 4.

Safety note: Ask an adult to operate the food processor for you.

Cold fish with rice

You will need:

1 large whole fish (about 1-1½ kg) such as cod or bass, gutted and scaled, but with the head intact

6 tablespoons of olive oil

1 large green pepper, seeded and chopped

2 medium onions, thinly sliced

3 cloves of garlic, crushed

6 medium tomatoes, skinned and sliced

1 tablespoon of tomato purée

a bunch of parsley, finely chopped

salt and pepper

6 whole green olives as garnish

What to do:

Rinse the fish and pat dry on kitchen paper. (1) If the skin is very thick, make several diagonal slits to aid the cooking. Heat the oil in a large frying pan and fry the fish very slowly. When it is golden on both sides, lift out, drain on kitchen paper and allow to cool. (2) Sauté the pepper in the same oil, add the onion after 10 minutes and cook until both are soft. Add garlic and sauté a further 2 minutes. Pulp the tomatoes and blend with the purée and parsley. Add to the pan, season to taste, stir well and simmer, stirring frequently for 15 minutes. (3) Lift the fish carefully back into the pan, cover with the sauce and cook gently for 15 minutes, or until tender. If the sauce is too thick, dilute with a little water and lemon juice. (4) Finally, lift the fish onto a large serving dish and spoon the sauce over it. Surround with boiled rice, olives to garnish, cool and refrigerate. Remove about 10 minutes before eating.
Serves 4.

with walnut and paprika sauce, eaten with plain boiled rice.

Persian recipes transform the common chicken into a dish fit for a sheikh, or king, by using elaborate fruit stuffings (see chicken recipe on page 32). *Fesanjan*, baked duck served with walnut and pomegranate sauce, is prepared on very special occasions.

Seafood is widely eaten in the Middle East. The Arab states, in particular, have an abundance of fish and crustaceans. Served hot or cold, baked fish is a traditional feast. Prawn curries are popular in the Gulf States.

The Lebanese, Egyptians and

Persian chicken, a popular dish in Iran. Local recipes often combine meat and poultry with fruits.

Iraqis are great fish-eaters. The Mediterranean red mullet, or *rouget*, is popular in Beirut; people living along the Nile enjoy freshwater perch. *Mashgouf* is a traditional fish dish in Iraq, especially in restaurants near the Tigris river in the capital, Baghdad. A tasty carp-like fish, it is smoked on stakes around a fire.

The tangy taste of garlic, lemon-juice and olive oil dressing is characteristic of salads in the Middle East. A crisp, fresh salad – usually lettuce, onion and tomato – is served with every meal. Chilled salads, such as spinach or

Salata arabieh

You will need:
6 medium tomatoes, diced
1 large cucumber, peeled, rinsed and
   diced
2 medium onions, finely chopped
2 cloves of garlic, finely chopped
1 medium green pepper, seeded and
   diced
4 tablespoons of mint, chopped
4 tablespoons of parsley, finely
chopped
juice of 1-2 lemons
4-5 tablespoons of olive oil
salt and freshly ground pepper

What to do:
Combine all the vegetables in a bowl. Mix the remaining ingredients together in a cup and pour over the salad. Toss well and chill before serving.
Serves 6.

Persian chicken

You will need:

2 kg chicken
2 medium onions, finely chopped
120 g of butter
60 g of raisins
180 g of dried prunes, soaked and
    stoned
180 g of dried apricots, soaked and
    sliced
1 teaspoon of ground cinnamon
salt and freshly ground pepper

What to do:

(1) Sauté the onion in half the butter for a few minutes, add the fruits and sauté gently a further 10 minutes. Add the cinnamon, season and allow to cool. Heat the oven to 190°C/375°F/gas mark 5. (2) Meanwhile stuff the chicken with the fruit, (3) sewing the neck flap to keep the mixture in. Rub the bird with remaining butter, salt and pepper, wrap in foil and bake until tender (about 1½-2 hours). (4) Open the foil for the final 40 minutes so the skin will crispen.

Serves 6.

Ask an adult to show you how to stuff the chicken.

Safety note: Always be very careful when cooking with hot fat. Ask an adult to help. Also, ask an adult to take the chicken out of the oven for you.

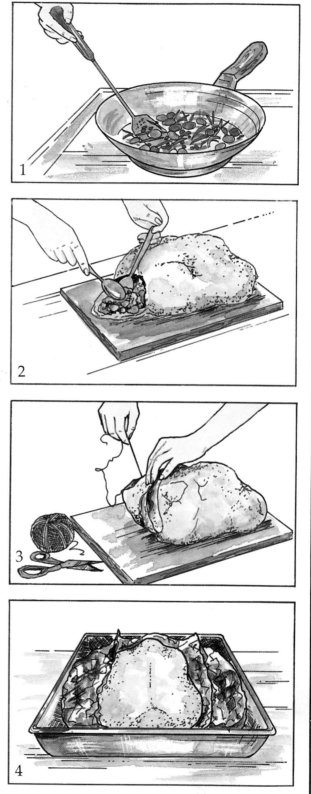

aubergine cooked with yoghurt, are also popular. So too are lentil salads and casseroles (*foul medames*) eaten by peasants, especially the *felaheen*, or farmers in Egypt.

A contrast to the savoury tastes of *mezze* are rich desserts and sweetmeats which, with fruit, usually end a typical Middle Eastern dinner.

The most common desserts are based on milk, semolina and rice flavoured with spices and rose-water or orange blossom water. Ground rice pudding, or *muhallabia* is a traditional dessert. Sweet saffron rice with nuts, raisins and peel is an Arab favourite.

In a long list of sweetmeats *baklava* is one of the best loved. Attributed to Palestinian cooks, *knaffeh* is also popular. A soft tart of

A selection of sweetmeats in a shop in Aleppo, Syria. Osh il bul-bul (left) and m'broume (centre) are filled with nuts.

crisp vermicelli filled with cream cheese, it is sold warm, from large, round baking trays.

Dazzling displays are a feature of pastry shops. Among pyramids of sweetmeats are always found *kataifi* (shredded nut pastries), *osh il bul-bul* (round pastry balls filled with ground nuts, like tiny birds' nests) and *ma'amoule*, bite-size pastries containing marzipan, or puréed dates.

The most widely eaten fruits are oranges, melons, bananas, peaches, grapes and dates (a single palm can yield as much as 150-300 kg). Dates feature in many aspects of Middle Eastern food and drink; the best come from Basra, in southern Iraq and from Nizwa, in Oman.

Typical Egyptian food: foule, *right of picture,* taamyeh *and* hummus, *rear. Flat bread is used to help oneself.*

Muhallabia (ground rice pudding)

You will need:

1 l of milk
2 tablespoons of ground rice
1 tablespoon of cornflour
5 tablespoons of sugar
1 tablespoon of rose-water
70 g of ground almonds
chopped, blanched almonds, or
   pistachio nuts, to garnish
grated nutmeg to sprinkle on top

What to do:

(1) Using a little of the milk, mix the ground rice and cornflour to a smooth paste. Slowly heat the sugar in the rest of the milk. (2) Add the paste, stirring continuously with a wooden spoon. Simmer the mixture until just off boiling point, being very careful not to burn the bottom of the pan as this will ruin the flavour. The mixture should thicken in 10-15 minutes. (3) Add the rose-water and ground almonds and continue to stir in the same direction over a low heat. Simmer for about 5 minutes, then remove and allow to cool slightly before pouring into a glass bowl, or individual glass dishes. (4) Garnish with the nuts and nutmeg, then chill for 3-4 hours before serving.

Drinks

Grapes have been cultivated in the Middle East since biblical times, but the consumption of wine, or any alcohol, is forbidden to Muslims.

People commonly drink mineral water, or yoghurt and water with meals. Refreshing drinks at other times are orange, lemon and tamarind juices. The ancient Persians were masters at making *sharbats* (or sherbets) from limes, apricots and pomegranates.

Having an abundance of fruits poses no problems for countries such as Iran, Jordan, Syria and Lebanon. Until recently, however, the arid Arab states had only camel or goats' milk as an alternative to water. For Bedouin nomads, only water was available and water-rights at desert wells were a frequent cause of tribal feuds.

The recent wealth from oil and gas has enabled some Arab countries to bottle local mineral water supplies. And a change from the old days when *suqs* stocked only

Bedouin children drinking camel milk in the Arabian Gulf.

Indian mangoes, or bananas, modern supermarkets now sell all manner of tropical fruits as well as imported frozen soft fruits, strawberries and raspberries.

Hotels, such as the Gulf Hiltons, have devised exotic recipes for alternative drinks, or drinks without alcohol. Equipped with modern electric blenders, local cooks are experimenting with new ideas for beverages based on soft fruits, pineapples, bananas, passion fruit and coconut juice.

The two traditional hot beverages are tea, often spiked with ginger of cinnamon, and coffee. 'Mocha coffee' which was exported from the old seaport in North Yemen, had the most famous reputation in the world. Unfortunately this thick, black type of coffee, known as 'Turkish coffee' by Westerners, is rare today. The high prices of beans have put many traditional Middle Eastern coffee–houses out of business.

Qahwa (Arab coffee) uses coffee grounds, and the addition of cardamom pods gives the brew its distinctive flavour. Grinding the beans, brewing and serving the coffee is a complex ritual in traditional Arab society, in particular among the Bedouin.

Townsfolk observe similar customs. The first cup of coffee is offered to the host. This assures a guest it is safe to drink although, by tradition, it is considered the

Limoonada

You will need:
Juice of 10 lemons or 20 green limes
Sugar syrup to taste
1-2 teaspoons of orange blossom water (available from Indian, Greek or Lebanese grocery stores)
¼ cup of freshly chopped mint (for the garnish)
Crushed ice

What to do:
(1) Mix the ingredients in a pitcher together with the crushed ice. Serve in individual glasses, topped up with soda, lemonade or Seven Up. (2) Garnish each glass with a sprig of mint.

The Qur'an forbids the consumption of alcohol. Here a Qatari enjoys a strawberry milkshake instead.

'unworthy cup'.

The second cup is poured by the bearer who holds the pot in his left hand, and a stack of cups in his right palm. The cup is handed to the visitor whose acceptance of it indicates his satisfaction with the hospitality.

The bearer will stand attentively, waiting for the cup to be held out for more. It is usual to drink at least three to four cups; a silent flick of the cup signifies that one has had enough.

Hospitality is second nature in Middle Eastern society. Meetings always begin with a visitor being offered coffee, tea or other beverage. Real business does not start until this is over. Likewise, refreshments and food are always sent out to a driver.

There are three ways of ordering coffee in Arabic: sweet (*helou*, or *sukkar ziada*), medium (*mazbout*) or without sugar (*murra*). The

37

following recipe is for medium coffee.

A Middle Eastern coffee-house is the hub of local male society, similar to a working man's pub in other countries.

Men meet here to gossip – a coffee-house is the first to know of any news – and to play a game of cards, or *tric-trac* (a game like dominoes which is said to have been invented in Mesopotamia).

The waiter, usually a young boy, keeps up a constant supply of tea or coffee, while a bearer, usually an elderly man, attends to the preparation of a *nargila*, or water-pipe. This is often shared and the gentle bubbling in the glass bowl adds to the relaxed atmosphere of the coffee-house.

Coffee is ritually offered at every opportunity. The host is seated on the left.

Turkish Coffee

You will need:
3 tablespoons of roasted ground coffee
1 heaped teaspoon of sugar
2 small coffee cups of water
tiny pinch of ground cinnamon

What to do:
Combine all the ingredients in a long-handled coffee pot, or a tiny saucepan, stir well and bring to the boil. As froth forms on top, remove from the stove, stir again and return to the heat until the froth rises again. Ensure it does not boil over. Boil again briefly, then stand aside for a few seconds. Have the small cups ready to pour in the coffee, raising the pot (impossible with a saucepan) to put a nice froth on each cup. The grounds should be allowed to settle before the coffee is drunk.

Food for special occasions

Relatively few festivals are celebrated in Islam. The two main occasions are *Eid al Fitr*, a three-day holiday marking the end of *Ramadan* and *Eid al Adha*, a four-day holiday marking the end of the *Hajj*, or pilgrimage. In Iran, the new year, or *Now-Ruz* is a joyous time.

Fasting once a year is considered spiritually cleansing. Throughout *Ramadan*, the ninth month in the Muslim calendar, nothing is eaten, or drunk, between the hours of dawn and dusk. In many towns, the end of the day's fast is signalled

At the evening iftar, *or breakfast during* Ramadan, *people begin with something light such as juices, yoghurt and dates.*

by the firing of a cannon. Elsewhere, the daily schedule is supplied by the mosque.

The routine during *Ramadan* is to take a little light meal and refreshment before dawn prayers. After sunset, the fast is broken with dates and fruits, such as grapes, eaten with yoghurt and bread. The family then has a big meal, always soup, followed by a variety of meat,

39

A whole roast lamb baked for Eid al Fitr, *the holiday following the end of the* Ramadan *fast.*

fish, rice and salads and then sweetmeats. Quantities of tea are drunk – the long hours of not being able to drink often causes dehydration in the very hot climate.

Eid al Fitr commences with prayers in the mosque and the distribution of gifts to family and friends and alms to the poor (*Zakat al Fitr*). The afternoon meal is a huge eating occasion. Wealthy families will have a whole stuffed lamb, or chickens. This is eaten with rice, salads and other main courses, as many as six dishes. Desserts and special sweetmeats are eaten at *Eid*. Iraqis eat *kalacha* (pastries filled with dates or raisins and nuts), and *nahash*, a pie made from nuts, honey and filo pastry is popular in Syria. *Knaffeh* is popular everywhere and is usually bought at special take-away pastry shops.

People drink a wide range of beverages. Orange, carrot and pomegranate sherbets are popular in Iraq and Iran. The Arabs are fond of bottled, soft drinks. Poor Bedouin refresh themselves with yoghurt and water.

Camel-racing, horseraces and aquatic regattas are held during the *Eid al Fitr* holiday when buildings and mosques are illuminated with festive lights.

Eid al Adha, or the 'feast of sacrifice', marks the end of the pilgrimage to Makkah during *Zul-Hijja*, the last month of the Muslim calendar. Every Muslim who can afford it, must slaughter an animal. Christians may not approve, but the event has deep

Camel races are popular entertainment during religious holidays in the Arab countries.

spiritual significance to a Muslim. An animal is symbolic of his willingness to sacrifice his dearest possession. The sacrifice also causes money to pass between the poor, who raise the animals, and the rich, who buy them and who often pay much more than its normal market price, in the name of Allah.

Strict rules are observed. The animals – sheep, goats or even a camel – must be killed on any of the three days after the special congregational prayers on *Eid*. The meat is then divided into equal portions: the first for the poor, the second for relatives and friends, and the third to be cooked at home by the household that made the sacrifice.

Children look forward to *Eid* as eagerly as Christian children do Christmas. They receive new clothes, toys and gifts, mainly money. Events such as children's birthdays are also celebrated in much the same way as in the West with present giving and a party.

Animals are ritually sacrificed at Eid al Adha *following the pilgrimage to Makkah. In the picture men are buying goats off a truck in Sohar, northern Oman.*

Western foods such as sandwiches and jellies have crept in among traditional *boreks* (crescent-shaped pastries filled with meat, or spinach and cheese), kebabs and other *mezze*. A birthday cake also follows the theme of a sponge, or similar type of cake.

Now-Ruz, the Persian new year, falls on 21 March, the first official day of spring. The occasion is marked by ceremony and feasting, a custom said to pre-date Islam.

About ten days before *Now-Ruz*, celebrations to emphasize the start of the new cycle begin with planting grains. The shoots are picked on the eve of *Now-Ruz* and divided among the family. Tied with ribbons, each bunch is put on a special table, or *haftsin* on which are also arranged seven items symbolizing the roots of life. Each begins with the letter 's': *sabzi* (herbs), *sir* (garlic), *sib* (apples), *sarkh* (vinegar), *sekeh* (coins), *samanoo* (pudding) and *sumak* (a crystalline lemon-tasting spice). Other things on the table are a bowl of water with a leaf floating in it, fruits, meat, fish, eggs, poultry, nuts, sweetmeats and the various grains to symbolize a bountiful harvest in the year ahead.

A copy of the Qur'an, candles, a mirror and a bowl of goldfish are other traditional items placed on the *haftsin*.

Superstition says it brings bad luck to stay indoors on the thirteenth day of *Now-Ruz*. On this

Boreks, filo *pastry cases filled with minced meat or cheese and spinach, are traditional at a celebration.*

day, every able-bodied Iranian takes off from home.

The bunch of shoots is attached to the front of the family car, to be later untied and flung into a stream. Quantities of food for a picnic are packed – things like stuffed cabbage leaves, cold herb and nut omelette, kebabs, chicken and almond and coconut sweetmeats. Tea is taken along in silver samovars, or, more recently, in Western-type thermos flasks. All along the roadsides families are to be seen sitting on rugs spread on the ground – the women gossiping among themselves, the men chatting quietly together, the children playing nearby and everyone eating.

Middle Eastern food abroad

The past decade has seen many Middle Eastern restaurants, in particular Lebanese restaurants, open abroad. The reason is twofold.

First is the long civil war in Lebanon, a beautiful country which many considered the gastronomic centre of the Middle East. Thousands of Lebanese have now fled the country, taking their cuisine with them. Where large numbers have settled – in Paris, Sydney and Los Angeles there are now excellent restaurants to enjoy Middle Eastern food. In fact there is scarcely a city in the Western world or Africa, which does not display a sign somewhere saying 'Lebanese Cuisine'.

In another way, the new oil and gas industry in the Arab countries has influenced the spread of Middle Eastern food abroad. Enormous

Middle Eastern food has travelled with migrants to the far corners of the world. Emad's is a popular Lebanese restaurant in Sydney, Australia.

wealth shared by the oil-generation of Arabs, enables even the Bedouin to take a holiday overseas. The first tourists actually brought their own sheep to slaughter and cooks to prepare their meals according to Qur'anic requirements. Profiting from this new market, leading European hotels began employing Muslim chefs to prepare typical menus. Before long, Westerners became familiar with Middle Eastern foods.

It is now common to find *hummus* served at London cocktail parties, *shawarma* sizzles in Gloucester Road snackbars while *falafel* bubbles in take-aways around Piccadilly.

Edgeware Road with its Middle Eastern restaurants and food stores, news stands and real estate agents is considered to be London's "Little Arabia".

If you have trouble obtaining any cooking ingredients where you live, try your local Greek, or Indian corner-store. *Ghee* and spices are available here while Greek, Cypriot or Turkish shops stock *laban* (strained yoghurt), cracked wheat and various fresh herbs such as coriander leaves.

An Arab family on holiday to London. The airline serves local Middle Eastern food on the menu.

Appendix

The following are Arabic translations of the most commonly used spices in cooking:

Allspice	*bahar*
Anise	*anisum*
Black pepper	*fil-fil afwad*
Cardamom	*hayl (habahan)*
Chilli	*fil-fil ahmar har*
Cloves	*kabsh qaranful*
Coriander	*kusbarah*
Cumin	*kammun*
Fenugreek	*helba*
Ginger	*zanjibil*
Mace	*fuljan*
Nutmeg	*jawz al-teeb*
Paprika	*fil-fil ahmar*
Saffron	*za'fran*
Sesame seed	*sim-sim*
Tamarind	*tammar al-Hindi*
Tumeric	*kurkum*

Spices are an essential ingredient in Middle Eastern cooking.

Glossary

Arabs People originally inhabiting Arabia who spread throughout the Middle East as well as North Africa and Spain in the seventh and eighth centuries AD.

Baklava A syrup sweetmeat made of filo pastry stuffed with crushed nuts.

Bas-reliefs Sculptures which only slightly project from their background but no part is actually detached from it.

Calamares Squid.

Caliphate A government ruled by the caliph, a title given to the acknowledged successors to Muhammad. The first caliphate was the Ummayad ruling from Damascus in AD 660.

Clarified To make clear, or pure, by removing suspended particles.

Cholesterol A fatty substance

which is naturally present in the body in small amounts.

Co-operative projects Communal projects where several people are involved in a common ideal.

Culinary Relating to, or used in, the kitchen or in cookery.

Dehydration To become parched through loss of water and insufficient intake of fluids.

De-salination To remove salt from sea-water to make pure water.

Etiquette The unwritten rules of correct behaviour.

Hydroponic A method of cultivation by growing plants in a solution instead of soil.

Illiterate Unable to read and write.

Knaffeh A shredded vermicelli sweetmeat filled with cream cheese.

Koubz Flat, unleavened, Arab bread.

Mezze Hors d'oeuvres or a variety of appetizers.

Myrrh A valuable resin used medically and as incense.

Nationalism Loyalty or devotion to one's country.

Offal The nutritious insides of an animal such as the heart, liver, brains and kidneys.

Pastoral nomadism People practising some form of cultivation on the move.

Pulses Beans, peas and similar edible seeds.

Quern A millstone used for grinding grain, usually wheat.

Qur'an The sacred script of Islam. It is the collected pronouncements of the Prophet Muhammad and is the basic source of guidance for daily living for Muslims.

Seasonal migration An annual migration, or movement, from place to place relating to climatic change and often involving a change in altitude.

Sovereign state A state independent of outside authority.

Subsistence farming Cultivation by a farmer for his own consumption and that of his family.

Suq A bazaar or market in a Middle Eastern town.

Urbanization Mode of life in a large town or city as opposed to a smaller town.

Picture acknowledgements

Michael Holford 8, Hutchison Library 35, 40(bottom). **All other photographs were supplied by Christine Osborne.** The publishers would like to thank the above for their permission to reproduce copyright pictures. The map on page 5 is by Malcolm Walker. All step-by-step recipe illustrations are by Juliette Nicholson.

Further reading

Ahsan, M.M., *Muslim Festivals* (Wayland, 1985)

Benghiat, Suzy, *Middle East Cookery* (St. Michael, 1984)

Dosti, Rose, *Middle East Cooking* (HP Books, 1982)

Hatin, M. Abdel-Kader, *Land of the Arabs* (Longman, 1977)

Kristensen, P., and Cameron, Fiona, *We Live in Egypt* (Wayland, 1986)

Latif al Hoad, Abdul, *We Live in Saudi Arabia* (Wayland, 1986)

Mallos, Tess, *The Complete Middle East Cookbook* (Summit, 1979)

Osborne, Christine, *An Insight and Guide to Jordan* (Longman, 1981)

Osborne, Christine, *People at work in the Middle East* (Batsford, 1987)

Osborne, Christine, *Cooking the Middle Eastern Way* (Admiral, 1985)

Roden, Claudia, *A Book of Middle Eastern Food* (Penguin, 1968)

Scott, David, *Traditional Arab Cookery* (Rider, 1983)

Index